SELF-ANALYSIS
FROM YOUR
HANDWRITING

SELF-ANALYSIS
FROM YOUR
HANDWRITING

ALBERT E. HUGHES

GROSSET & DUNLAP
A NATIONAL GENERAL COMPANY
Publishers · New York

A Castle Books, Inc. Edition
Distributed To The Trade
By Book Sales, Inc.

To the memory of
Dr. med. and Dr. phil.
George Strelisker

There is a principle which is a bar against all information, which is proof against all argument and which cannot fail to keep a man in everlasting ignorance. That principle is condemnation before investigation.

HERBERT SPENCER

CONTENTS

7

Chapter

23. SMALL LETTERS   65

24. THE LETTER "I"   67

25. THE LETTER "T"   72

26. INITIAL AND TERMINAL LETTERS   75

27. LOOPS IN THE LOWER ZONE   80

28. INTELLIGENCE   84

29. UNRELIABILITY AND DISHONESTY   85

30. TRAIT LIST   87

     RECORD OF A HANDWRITING ANALYSIS   91

     TABLE OF CHARACTERISTICS   92

     BIBLIOGRAPHY   95

ILLUSTRATIONS

Figure

PREFACE

Today, there are signs that graphology, the psychology of hand-writing, is at last receiving the consideration which it deserves. Feature articles appear in magazines, references appear on TV and on the cinema screen. Unfortunately, there are very few suitable books for the beginner. They are either detailed works for the specialist or they are irresponsible products for the sensation-seeker.

It is to be hoped that the following pages will fill a much-felt gap.

A. E. H.

Tweedside, Cheddon Fitzpaine
Taunton, Somerset

CHAPTER I

INTRODUCTION

Graphology, the science of handwriting, is a psycho-diagnostic aid which has not yet been accepted by British universities as a suitable "scientific" discipline. Graphology is an aspect of characterology and this subject is equally ignored by our universities. However, in German-speaking countries characterology and graphology are recognised. In universities in those countries graphology can be read for a degree and it always forms an integral part of any psychology course. So you see, graphology is more than a tent-and-crystal-ball pastime!

Aristotle showed an interest in graphology more than three hundred years before the birth of Christ. The Roman Emperor Justinian showed more than a passing interest in different handwritings. Nearer our own times, the first published work on graphology appeared in Bologna at the beginning of the seventeenth century and was entitled *Ideographia*. This was followed by Baldo's treatise in 1622. Since that date there have appeared many works in different languages.

Among French graphologists were Flandrin, Michon and Crépieux-Jamin. Michon coined the word "graphology" which is now accepted. He concentrated on studies of single letters but Crépieux-Jamin moved away from the "school of fixed signs" to studies of the over-all aspects of writing.

Among German graphologists were Preyer, Meyer, Klages, Kraepelin, Jacoby and Pophal. Preyer was a professor of physiology at Jena and he demonstrated that a script produced by either left or right hand or foot, or even by the mouth, of the same person possessed a similarity of writing pattern. Meyer was a psychiatrist who stressed three important factors of writing movement—extension, speed and pressure. He helped to develop a new science of characterology because he recognised that problems of expression are aspects of character. Klages developed a science of expression which postulated laws and principles governing graphology, expressive movement and characterology. He also taught that the basic law of expression is that each expressive physical movement actualises the tensions and drives of the personality. He stressed the importance of assessing by intuition the rhythm of a script and so arriving at the "form level". Kraepelin was a psychiatrist who devised the Kraepelin scale which attempts to measure writing speed and pressure in the scripts of both the mentally well and unwell. Pophal was appointed professor of neurology in Hamburg after the last war and he has carried out graphological research in terms of personality types as reflected in motor activity of the brain. Jacoby was a graphological practitioner of outstanding ability whose untimely death was a great loss.

In Switzerland Schlag has studied graphology in terms of Jung's analytical psychology while Pulver has studied the symbolism of the writing space.

Fanta, Menzel and Schönfeld were three Czech graphologists who, in 1939, launched a short-lived journal as an international forum for graphological discussion. There was also Saudek who attempted to deal with graphological phenomena in terms acceptable to the experimental psychologists.

In Hungary a graphological institute was founded in 1920. Notable among Hungarian graphologists have been Roman, Balázs and Hajnal. The two latter studied the subject in terms of psycho-analysis. Roman devised a "graphodyne" for measuring graphological phenomena.

In the United States graphology has received the attention of June Downey of the University of Iowa, as well as of Allport and Vernon of the Harvard Psychological Clinic. The two latter have attempted to make use of statistics and the experimental approach. A more clinical approach, making use of scales, has been made by Zubin and Lewinson and this was followed up by Rose Wolfson. Contemporary experimental graphology is investigated by Wolff and contemporary clinical graphology is investigated by Sonnemann.

Finally, mention must be made of my own teacher, the late Dr. George Strelisker, of Vienna and Berlin. He was both a graphologist and a cheirologist who served as a handwriting consultant to the Austrian police until 1937. His published work (listed in the bibliography) did not mention his researches on the "internal writing flow" which he related to the Jungian undifferentiated dimension. At this point, nothing more than a passing reference can be made about this most important (and hitherto completely unknown) aspect of graphology.

Before proceeding to graphological analysis, I must remind you that graphology, being a department of characterology, is concerned with characteristics. Now characteristics have two poles: positive and negative. So you will find at the end of this book a table of characteristics illustrating the principle of the "polarity of values". For example, tact (which is positive) can become deceit (which is negative). However, what decides whether we interpret characteristics positively or negatively is the "form level" and this is the subject of the next chapter.

CHAPTER 2

FORM LEVEL

The form level gives us an over-all impression of the writing. We assess the quality of the form level by considering:

(*a*) the distribution of spaces,
(*b*) the naturalness or artificiality of the script,
(*c*) the originality of the script.

As a result of these considerations we decide the quality of the form level as being:

(*a*) above average,
(*b*) average,
(*c*) below average.

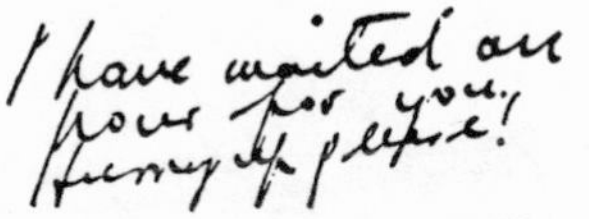

Fig. 1. *Distribution of spaces below average.*

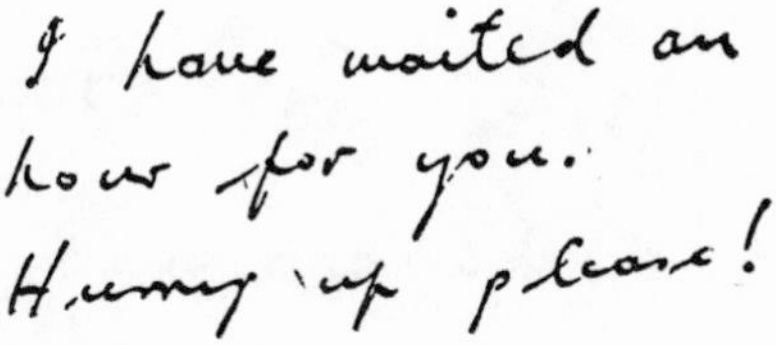

Fig. 2. *Distribution of spaces above average.*

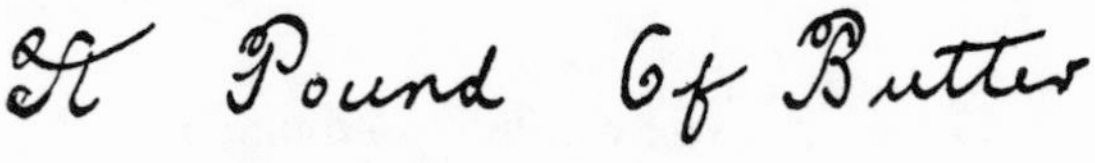

Fig. 3. *An artificial script.*

A Pound Of Butter

Fig. 4. A natural script.

A Pound Of Butter

Fig. 5. A script lacking in originality.

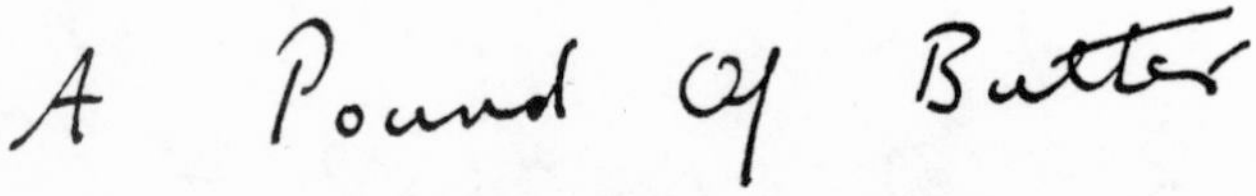

A Pound Of Butter

Fig. 6. A script exhibiting originality.

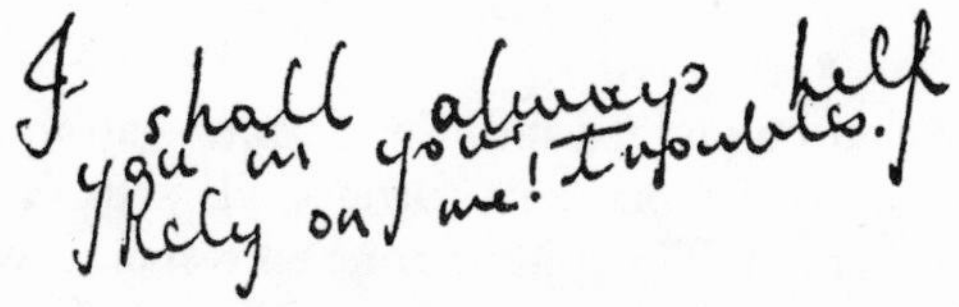

Fig. 7. A form level which is below average.

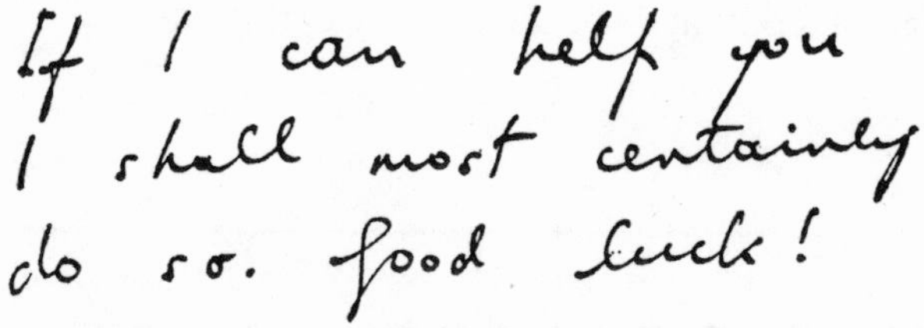

Fig. 8. A form level which is above average.

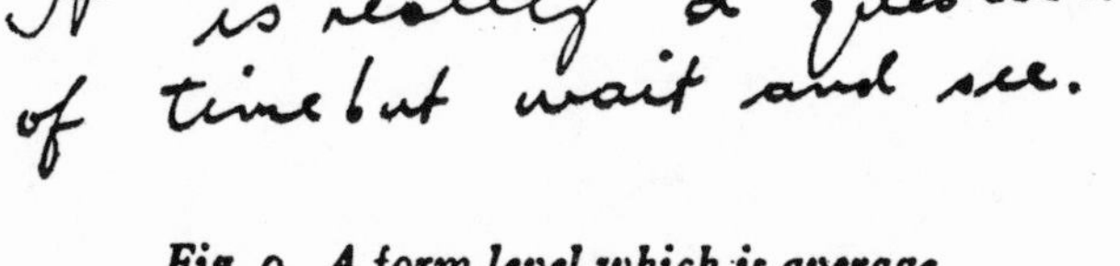

Fig. 9. A form level which is average.

CHAPTER 3

THE ZONES

Handwriting can be divided into three zones—an upper, middle and lower zone. The upper zone corresponds with Freud's super-ego or Jung's heaven. The middle zone corresponds with Freud's and Jung's ego. The lower zone corresponds to Freud's id and to Jung's personal and collective unconscious. The upper zone is therefore the realm of spirit, conscience or intellect. The middle zone is the world of the individual consciousness. The lower zone is the domain of instinct and materialism. According to the emphasis on the zone of a writing, the writer's predominant interests and attitudes can be evaluated.

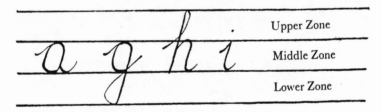

Fig. 10. The zones of a script.

CHAPTER 4

THE DIRECTIONS

The left direction of writing symbolises the past, the self and introversion. The right direction symbolises the future, other people and extroversion. The left direction also symbolises conservatism of mind and the head ruling the heart. The right direction symbolises radicalism and the heart ruling the head. Upright writing symbolises an independent nature. It must be remembered, however, that no writing is absolutely sloping in one particular direction. What is sought is the predominant slope.

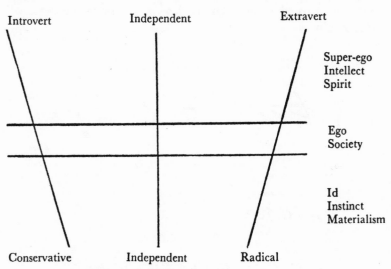

Fig. 11. The directions (left/right) and zones (upper, middle, lower) of handwriting.

CHAPTER 5

WIDTH AND NARROWNESS

A wide writing is one in which the distance between the down-strokes of small letters is greater than the height.

A narrow writing is one in which the distance between the downstrokes of small letters is less than the height.

A normal writing is one in which the distance between the downstrokes of small letters is equal to the height.

A wide writing symbolises extroversion, an outward movement towards society. The writer is uninhibited in personal relationships.

A narrow writing symbolises introversion, an inward movement towards the ego. The writer is inhibited in personal relationships.

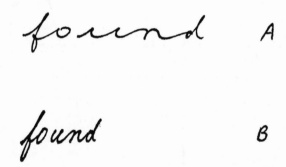

Fig. 12. A = wide writing, B = narrow writing

CHAPTER 6

THE SPACES BETWEEN WORDS AND LINES

The writer's distribution of spaces between words and lines is symbolic of his organisational abilities.

A wide script can be interpreted positively as orderliness of thinking or negatively as lack of spontaneity; or positively as generosity, negatively as lavishness; or positively as formality, negatively as isolation.

A narrow script can be interpreted positively as economy or negatively as avarice; or positively as spontaneity, negatively as instability; or positively as informality, negatively as familiarity.

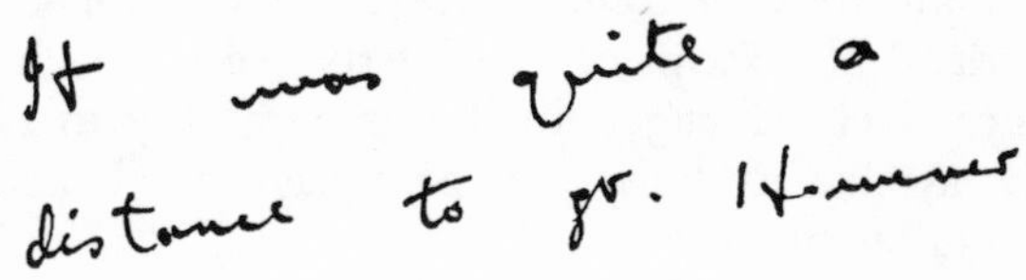

Fig. 13. A wide distribution of words and spaces.

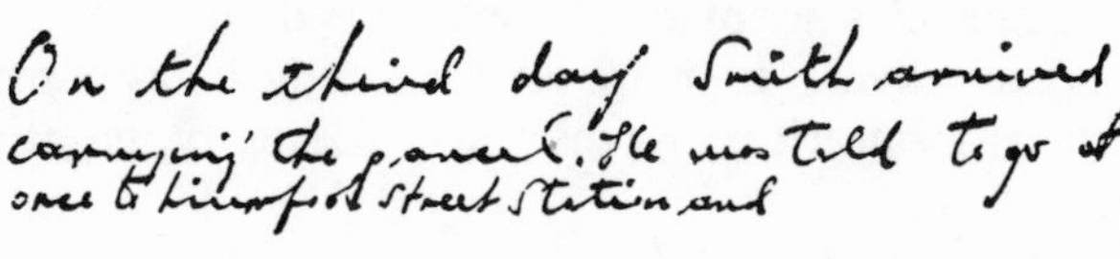

Fig. 14. A narrow distribution of words and spaces.

CHAPTER 7

CONNECTIONS

There are four main types of connection :

(a) arcade,
(b) garland,
(c) angle,
(d) thread.

The arcade form of connection symbolises reserve.

The arcades of a script can be interpreted positively as tactfulness or negatively as insincerity; or positively as reserve, negatively as distrust; or positively as formalism, negatively as mannerism.

The garland form of connection symbolises frankness.

The garland of a script can be interpreted positively as kindness or negatively as suggestibility; or positively as sympathy, negatively as distractability; or positively as tolerance, negatively as indifference.

The angular form of connection symbolises resistance.

The angles of a script can be interpreted positively as determination or negatively as rigidity; or positively as firmness, negatively as coldness; or positively as loyalty, negatively as an uncompromising nature.

The thready form of connection symbolises flexibility.

The threads of a script can be interpreted positively as excitability or negatively as hysteria; or positively as diplomacy, negatively as insincerity; or positively as dexterity, negatively as cunning.

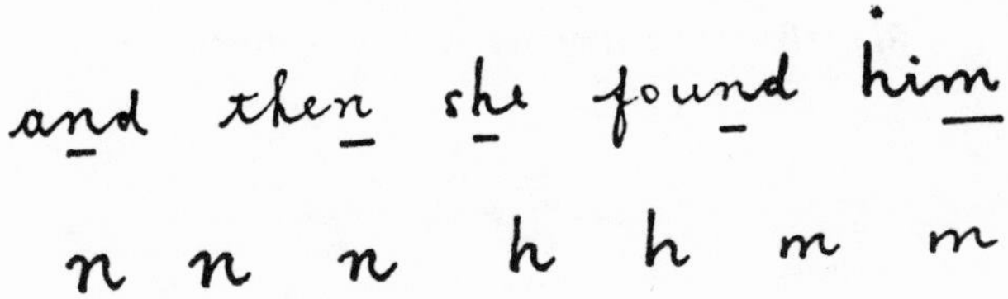

and then she found him

n n n h h m m

Fig. 15. The arcade form of connection.

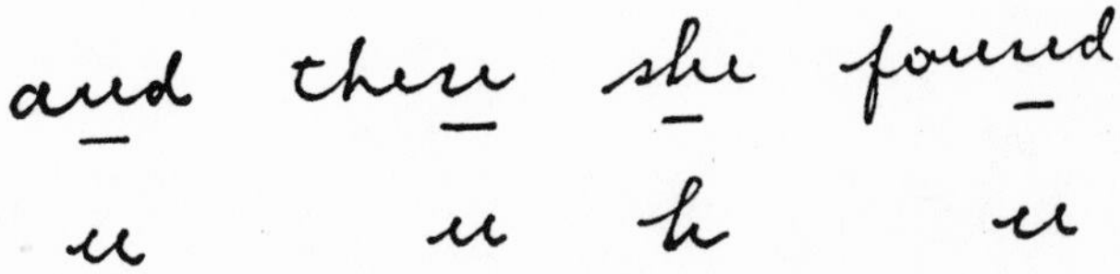

and then she found

u u h u

Fig. 16. The garland form of connection.

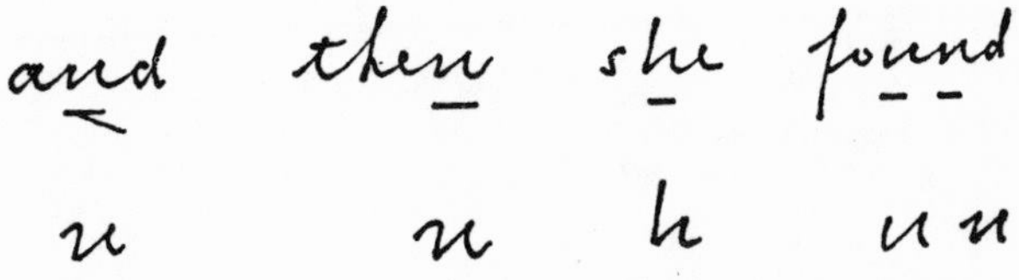

and then she found

u u h u u

Fig. 17. The angular form of connection.

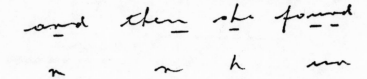

Fig. 18.   The thready form of connection.

CHAPTER 8

CONNECTEDNESS

A connected script is one in which five or more letters are written in one stroke. Breaks in the script caused by the dotting of a letter "i" or the crossing of a letter "t" do not count.

A disconnected script is one in which four or less letters are written in one stroke. Type script is not necessarily disconnected script.

A connected script can be interpreted positively as sociability or negatively as mass-mindedness; or positively as reproductive intelligence, negatively as lack of initiative; positively as speed of thought, negatively as superficiality of thought.

A disconnected script can be interpreted positively as intuitive thinking or negatively as lack of concentration; or positively as individualism, negatively as egocentricity; or positively as independence, negatively as unsociability.

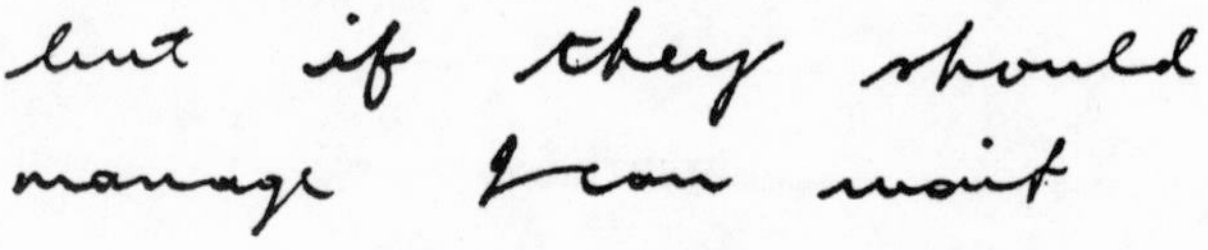

Fig. 19. A connected script.

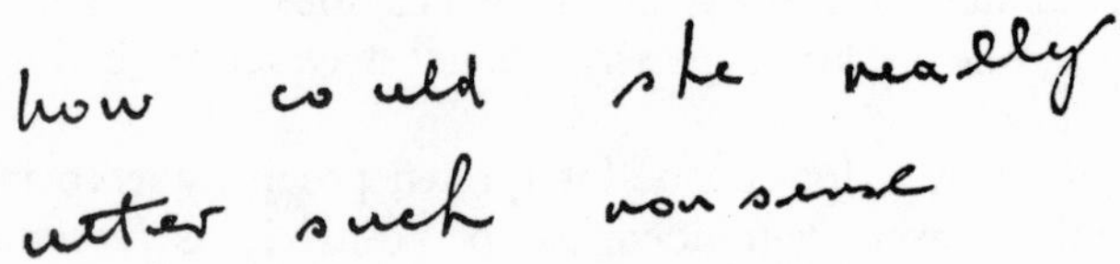

Fig. 20. A disconnected script.

CHAPTER 9

SLANT OF LETTERS

The vertical script symbolises neutrality. Such a script need not be at an angle to the writing line of exactly ninety degrees. Five degrees either way (eighty-five to ninety-five degrees) is considered a vertical script.

The vertical script can be interpreted positively as rationality or negatively as coldness; or positively as uncommittedness, negatively as indifference; or positively as self-control, negatively as rigidity.

The left-slanting script symbolises concern with one's ego. A script with a writing angle of sixty to eighty-five degrees is considered left-slanting. A writing angle of less than sixty degrees should be interpreted negatively.

The left-slanting script can be interpreted positively as an influence of tradition or negatively as fear of the future; or positively as self-control, negatively as artificiality; or positively as precaution, negatively as withdrawal.

The right-slanting script symbolises concern with society. A script with a writing angle of one hundred and forty-five degrees is considered right-slanting. A writing angle of more than one hundred and forty-five degrees should be interpreted negatively.

The right-slanting script can be interpreted positively as sociability or negatively as mass-mindedness; or positively as passion, negatively as emotional extravagance; or positively as progressiveness, negatively as radicalism.

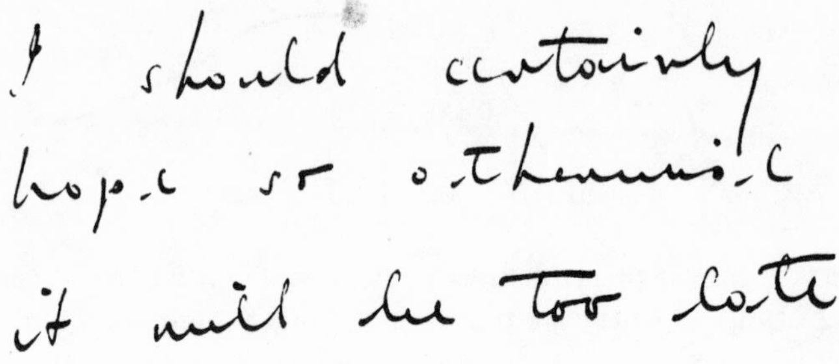

*I should certainly
hope so otherwise
it will be too late*

Fig. 21. A vertical script.

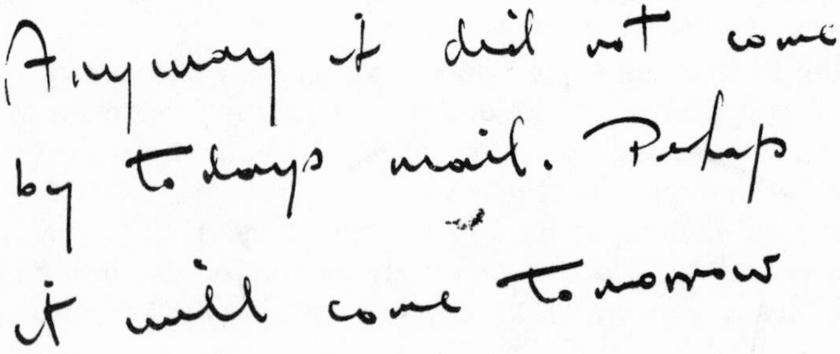

*Anyway it did not come
by todays mail. Perhaps
it will come tomorrow*

Fig. 22. A left-vertical script.

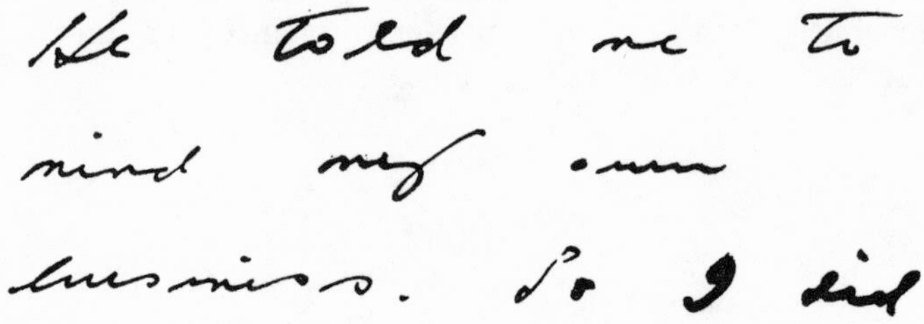

*He told me to
mind my own
business. So I did*

Fig. 23. A right-slanting script.

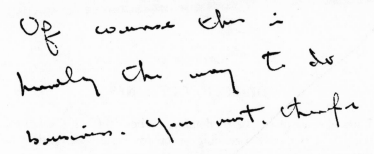

Fig. 24. A left-slanting script.

CHAPTER 10

DIRECTION OF LINES

Lines of a script can be predominantly horizontal in their direction, predominantly ascending or predominantly descending in their directions.

Any script may exhibit moods of the moment peculiar to the particular writer. The directions of lines, especially, may indicate emotional conditions obtaining only at the time when the script was written. On the other hand, they may signify condiions which are more permanent. A thorough study of the writing as a whole will determine the interpretation accordingly.

Ascending lines may be interpreted positively as enthusiasm or negatively as excitability; or positively as energy, negatively as restlessness; or positively as optimism, negatively as lack of a sense of reality.

Horizontal lines may be interpreted positively as constancy or negatively as dullness; or positively as emotional control, negatively as lack of feeling; or positively as method, negatively as pedantry.

Descending lines may be interpreted positively as fatigue or negatively as feebleness of will; or positively as pessimism, negatively as depression.

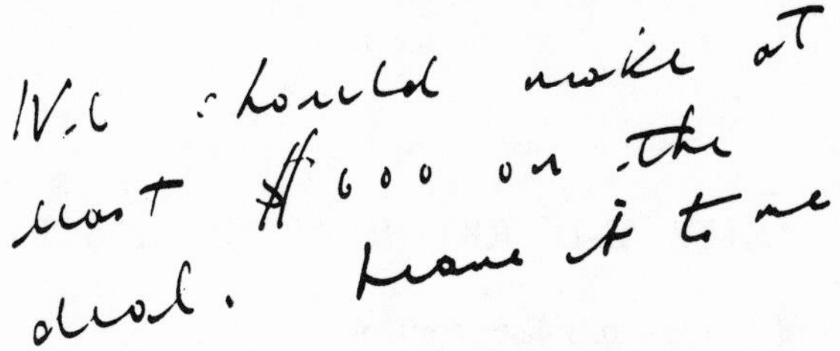

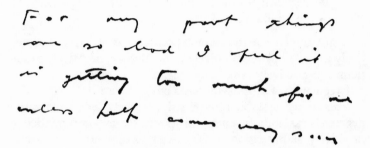

Fig. 25. An ascending script.

Fig. 26. A descending script.

CHAPTER II

REGULARITY AND IRREGULARITY OF SCRIPT

Regularity of script symbolises control.
It is determined by:

(a) the regularity of slant,
(b) the regularity of the height of downstrokes in the middle zone,
(c) the regularity of the height and the distance of downstrokes in the middle zone.

Regularity can be interpreted positively as orderliness or negatively as pedantry; or positively as endurance, negatively as fanaticism; or positively as stability, negatively as rigidity.

Irregularity of script symbolises emotionalism.

Irregularity can be interpreted positively as spontaneity or negatively as impulsiveness; or positively as open-mindedness, negatively as indecision; or positively as elasticity, negatively as inconstancy.

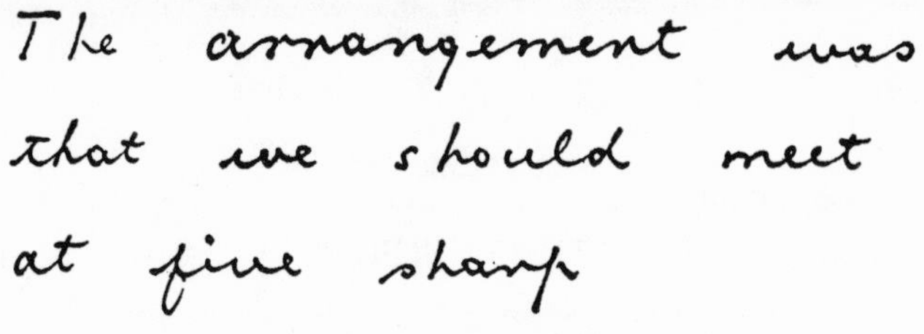

The arrangement was that we should meet at five sharp

Fig. 27. A regular script.

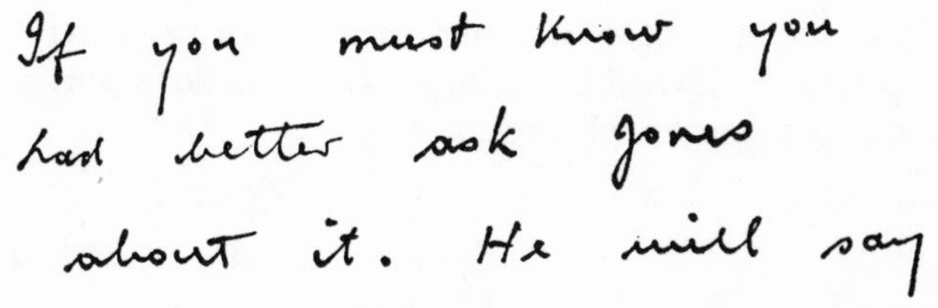

If you must know you had better ask jones about it. He will say

Fig. 28. A slightly irregular script.

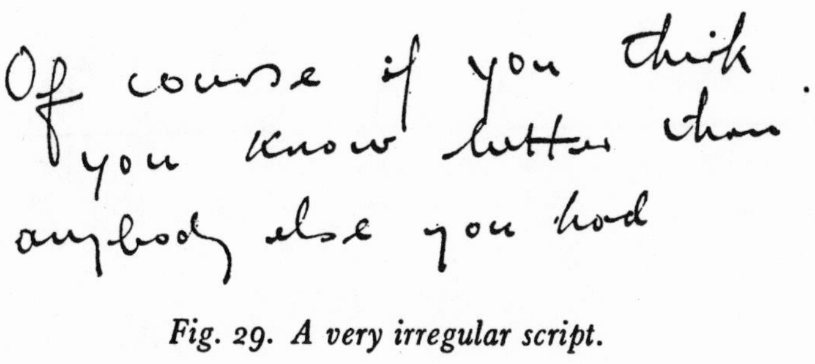

Of course if you think you know better than anybody else you had

Fig. 29. A very irregular script.

CHAPTER 12

SIZE OF SCRIPT

The size of a script symbolises the writer's assessment of himself.

It is determined by the size of the small letters which are about one-eighth of an inch (about three mm.).

A large size symbolises positively pride or negatively pomp; or positively generosity, negatively extravagance; or positively self-reliance, negatively asociality.

A small size symbolises positively modesty or negatively timidity; or positively respectfulness, negatively traditionalism; or positively tolerance, negatively indifference.

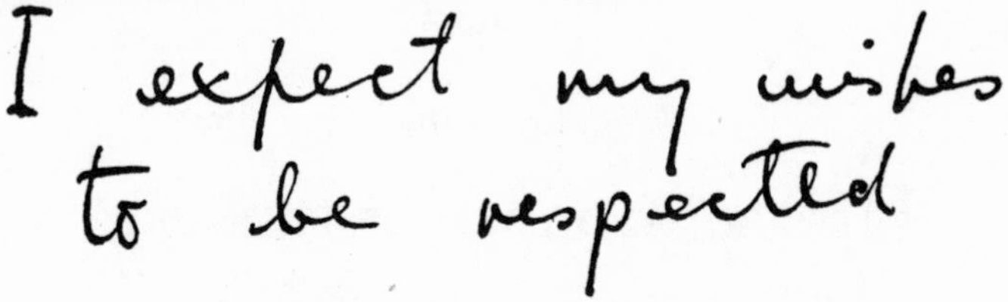

I expect my wishes to be respected

Fig. 30. A large script.

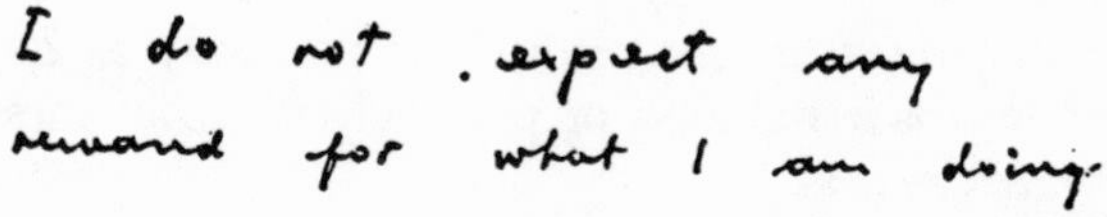

I do not expect any reward for what I am doing

Fig. 31. A small script.

CHAPTER 13

PRESSURE AND LACK OF PRESSURE

Pressure in a script symbolises libido or energy.

In a regular script pressure can be interpreted positively as endurance or negatively as obstinacy; or positively as steadiness, negatively as heaviness; or positively as masculinity, negatively as clumsiness.

In an irregular script pressure can be interpreted positively as vitality or negatively as excitability; or positively as impulsiveness, negatively as irritability; or positively as resoluteness, negatively as aggressiveness.

Lack of pressure in a script symbolises lack of libido or lack of energy.

In a regular script lack of pressure can be interpreted positively as adaptability or negatively as unsteadiness; or positively as elasticity, negatively as lack of resistance; or positively as femininity, negatively as yieldingness.

In an irregular script lack of pressure can be interpreted positively as dreaminess or negatively as distraction; or positively as impressionability, negatively as superficiality; or positively as sensitivity, negatively as weakness.

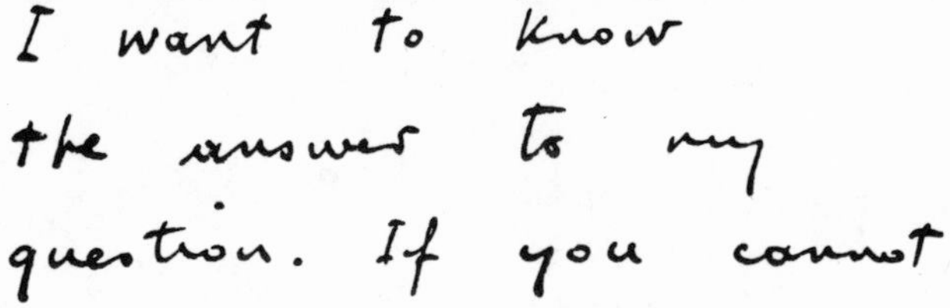

*I want to know
the answer to my
question. If you cannot*

Fig. 32. *Pressure in a regular script.*

*This sort of situation
should never have arisen.
They have wasted our
time.*

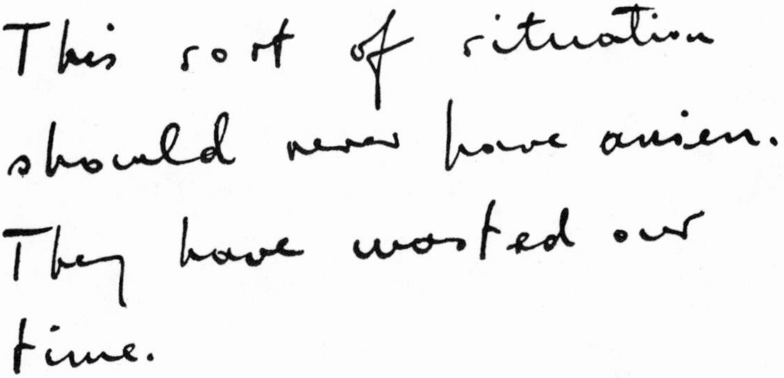

Fig. 33. *Pressure in an irregular script.*

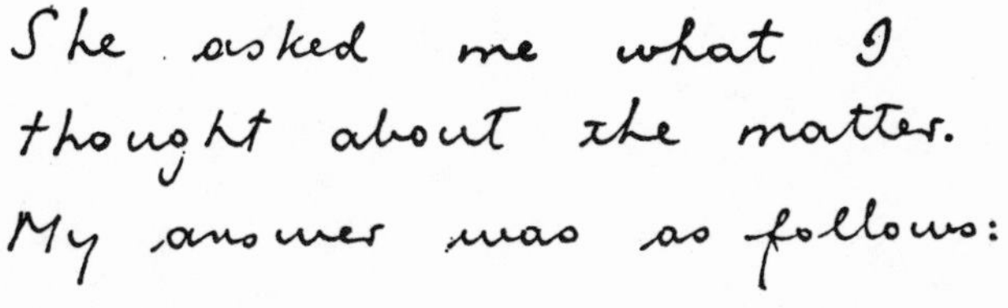

*She asked me what I
thought about the matter.
My answer was as follows:*

Fig. 34. *Lack of pressure in a regular script.*

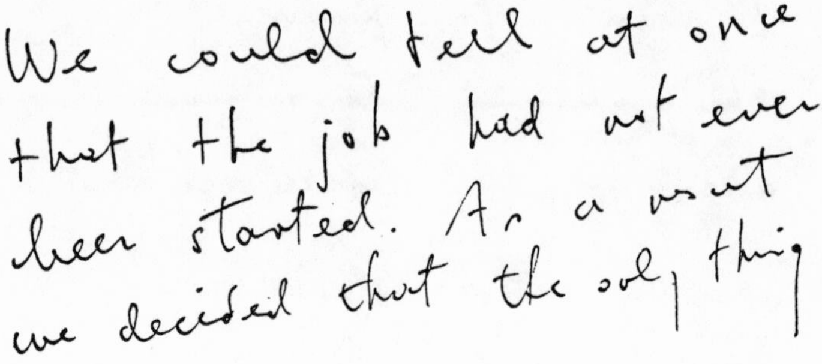

We could tell at once
that the job had not even
been started. As a result
we decided that the only thing

Fig. 35. *Lack of pressure in an irregular script.*

CHAPTER 14

PASTINESS AND SHARPNESS

Pastiness * in a script symbolises materialism.

It is produced by holding the pen at an angle of considerably less than ninety degrees. Consequently, the writing is produced by the flat of the nib as opposed to the point of the nib.

In a pasty script the upstrokes and downstrokes have the same thickness and they are never less than one-fiftieth of an inch.

Pastiness can be interpreted positively as naturalness or negatively as earthiness; or positively as refined sensuality, negatively as crudeness; or positively as enjoyment of living, negatively as lack of spirituality.

Sharpness in a script symbolises rationality.

It is produced by holding the pen at an angle of nearly ninety degrees. Consequently the writing is produced by the point of the nib as opposed to the flat of the nib.

In a sharp script the upstrokes and downstrokes have different thicknesses and are not more than one-fiftieth of an inch.

Sharpness can be interpreted positively as spirituality or negatively as asceticism; or positively as analytical-mindedness, negatively as criticism; or positively as self-discipline, negatively as coldness.

---

* In graphology *pastiness* is the term used to describe a thick flat stroke.

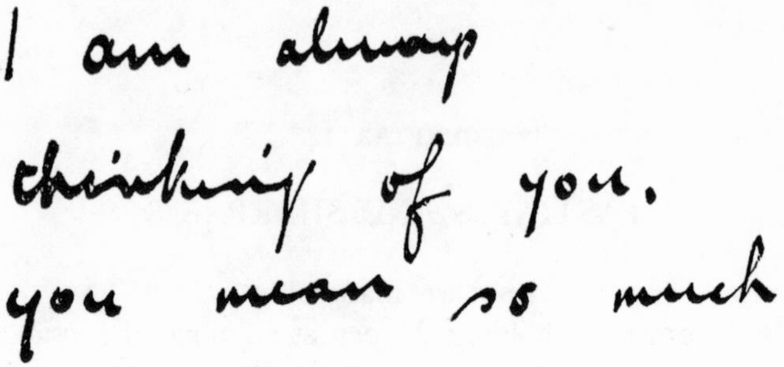

I am always
thinking of you.
you mean so much

Fig. 36. A pasty script.

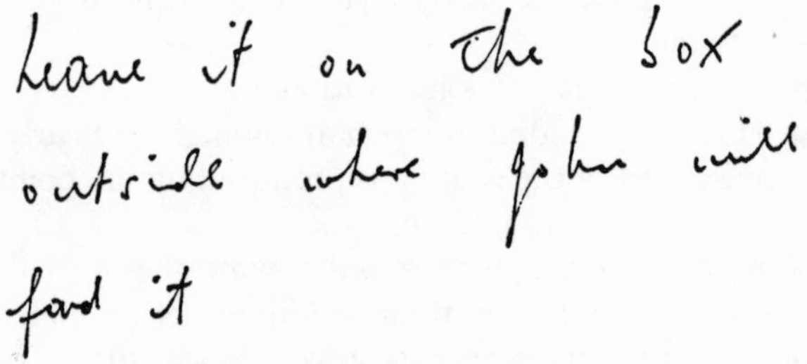

Leave it on the box
outside where john will
find it

Fig. 37. A sharp script.

CHAPTER 15

FULLNESS AND LEANNESS

A full script is one in which the letters (mainly the looped letters) are larger than the school pattern.

A lean script is one in which the letters (again, mainly the looped letters) are smaller than the school pattern.

Fullness in the upper zone can be interpreted positively as imagination or negatively as day-dreaming; or positively as vision, negatively as utopianism; or positively as colourful speech, negatively as bombast.

Leanness in the upper zone can be interpreted positively as analytical-mindedness or negatively as criticism; or positively as rationality, negatively as lack of imagination; or positively as ethical behaviour, negatively as ascetic behaviour.

Fullness in the middle zone can be interpreted positively as sociability or negatively as compulsive hospitality; or positively as warm nature, negatively as amiability; or positively as social success, negatively as social-climbing.

Leanness in the middle zone can be interpreted positively as social discrimination or negatively as snobbishness; or positively as emotional control, negatively as rigidity; or positively as coolness, negatively as coldness.

Fullness in the lower zone can be interpreted positively as countryside interests or negatively as earthiness; or positively as sensuousness, negatively as sensuality; or positively as erotic fantasies and behaviour, negatively as perverse fantasies and behaviour.

Leanness in the lower zone can be interpreted positively as sexual sublimation or negatively as sexual repression; or positively as realism, negatively as pessimism; or positively as ethical demands, negatively as a neurotically sharp conscience.

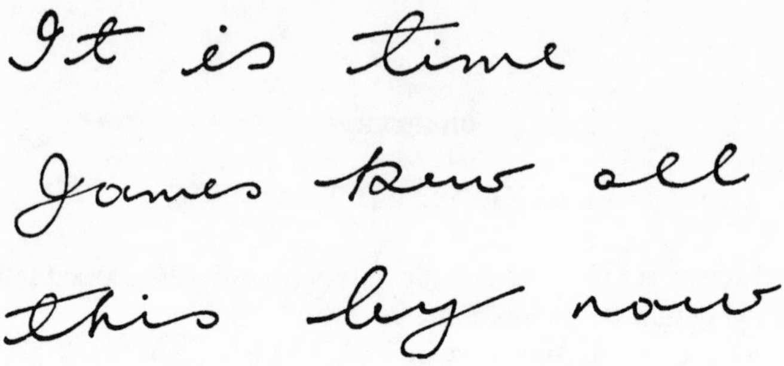

It is time
James knew all
this by now

Fig. 37A. A full script.

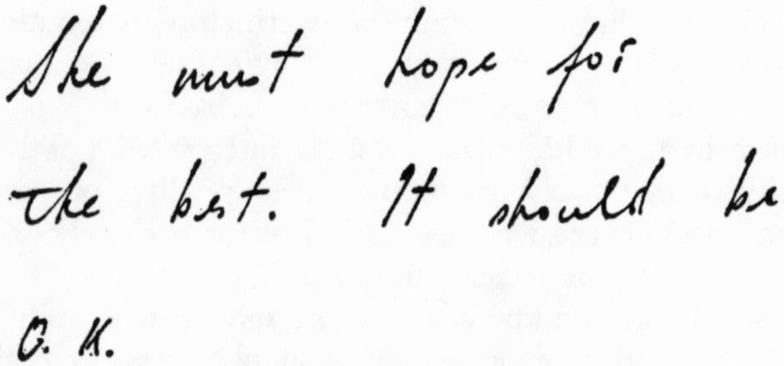

She must hope for
the best. It should be
O. K.

Fig. 38. A lean script.

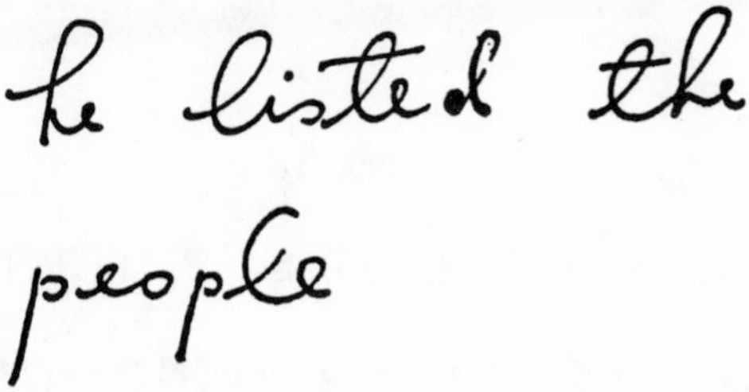

he listed the people

Fullness in upper middle zone, leanness in lower zone.

they all sat down together

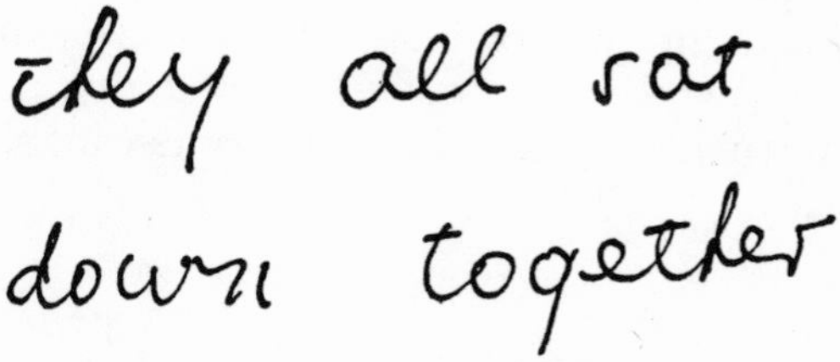

Fullness in middle zone, leanness in lower zone.

she got along

Fullness in lower zone.

Fig. 38A. Fullness and leanness in the zones.

CHAPTER 16

ORNAMENTATION AND SIMPLIFICATION

In an ornamental script there are additional flourishes which do not improve the legibility.

In a simplified script the letters are reduced to their basic form without impairing the legibility of the script.

An ornamental script can be interpreted positively as originality or negatively as affectation; or positively as pride, negatively as pomp; or positively as formality, negatively as vanity.

A simplified script can be interpreted positively as simplicity or negatively as neglect; or positively as maturity, negatively as lack of form sense; or positively as sense for essentials, negatively as unreliability.

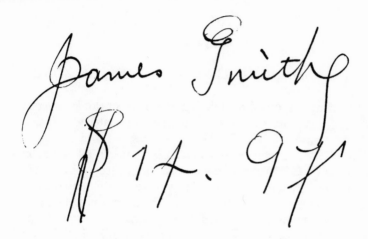

Fig. 39. Ornamentation.

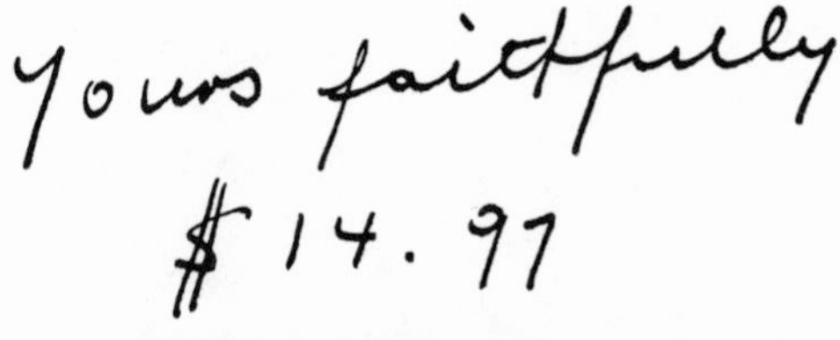

Fig. 40. Simplification.

CHAPTER 17

LEFT AND RIGHT TENDENCIES IN THE ZONES

Left tendencies symbolise inhibition, the inner world, introversion.

Right tendencies symbolise spontaneity, the outer world, extroversion.

These left and right tendencies can be found in all three zones of a script (that is to say, in the domain of intellect/spirit, society, the instincts). Again, both left and right tendencies may be found in one, two or three zones of a script. The determining factor will be the predominance of a particular tendency, for example, predominantly left or right. Thus, a script may exhibit both instinctual inhibition (left tendencies in the lower zone) and spiritual spontaneity (right tendencies in the upper zone). Yet the left tendencies in the lower zone may be more pronounced than the right tendencies in the upper zone. Such a writer would have a willing spirit but a weak flesh!

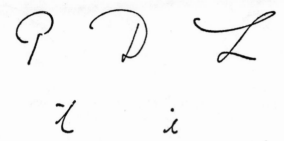

Fig. 41. *Left tendencies in the upper zone.*

Fig. 42. *Left tendencies in the middle zone.*

Fig. 43. *Left tendencies in the lower zone.*

Fig. 44. Right tendencies in the upper zone.

Fig. 45. Right tendencies in the middle zone.

Fig. 46. Right tendencies in the lower zone.

CHAPTER 18

SPEED

A speedy script is determined by :

- (a) rightward slant,
- (b) predominance of right tendencies,
- (c) ascending lines,
- (d) wide writing,
- (e) connectedness,
- (f) simplification,
- (g) good distribution of spaces,
- (h) naturalness,
- (i) originality,
- (j) dots of letter "i" and bars of letter "t" omitted or placed to the right,
- (k) garland or thready connection,
- (l) incompletion of final letters of words.

A slow script is determined by :

- (a) leftward slant,
- (b) predominance of left tendencies,
- (c) descending lines,
- (d) narrow writing,
- (e) disconnectedness,
- (f) ornamentation,
- (g) poor distribution of spaces,
- (h) artificiality,
- (i) lack of originality,
- (j) dots of letter "i" and bars of letter "t" omitted or placed to the left,
- (k) arcade or angular connections,
- (i) completion of final letters of words.

A speedy script can be interpreted positively as vivacity or negatively as escapism; or positively as naturalness, negatively as rashness; or positively as adaptability, negatively as superficiality.

A slow script can be interpreted positively as carefulness or negatively as nervousness; or positively as steadiness, negatively as inertia; or positively as thoughtfulness, negatively as slow thinking.

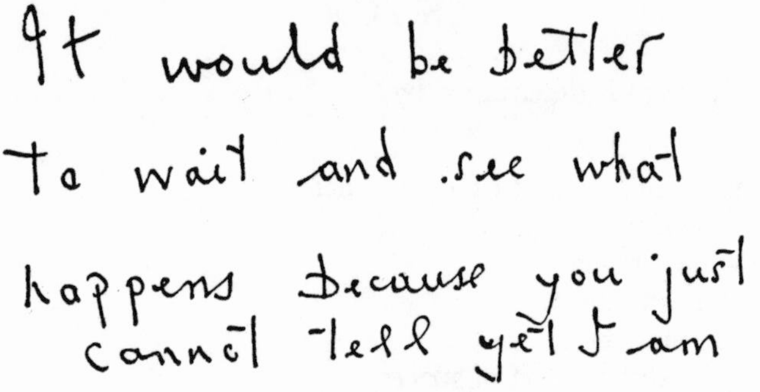

Fig. 47. A slow script.

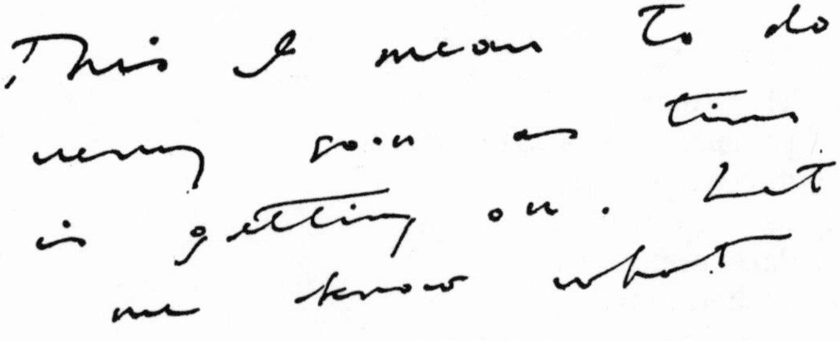

Fig. 48. A speedy script.

CHAPTER 19

MARGINS

The width of margins varies with the customs of the particular country. For example, German scripts tend to have a wide left margin, whereas American scripts often omit the left margin.

Left margins symbolise the past and the self.

Right margins symbolise the future and the world.

Wide margins indicate reserve or caution, narrow margins indicate informality or spontaneity.

If the four margins are equal in their widths this can be interpreted positively as good taste or negatively as artificiality.

If the four margins are missing this can be interpreted positively as broad-mindedness or negatively as vulgarity.

CHAPTER 20

SIGNATURES

The signature is the visiting card of the writer. More than any specimen of writing it symbolises the writer's ego.

Additional flourishes should be interpreted in terms of left and right tendencies in the different zones.

Underlinings, etc., emphasise the importance of the writer's ego.

Most signatures are illegible, especially those of professional people. But an illegible signature together with an illegible script should warn of a certain duplicity in the writer. However, a strikingly legible signature indicates either a rather uncomplicated type of writer or someone who is not called upon to sign his name very frequently or a person who would like to appear as a straightforward type of character. Again, it can be the signature of a pedant.

If the size of the signature is equal to that of the script it indicates a rather placid type of personality. If it is larger it indicates that the writer possesses more private than public confidence. If it is smaller the writer has more public than private confidence.

A signature written in the same style of writing as the body of the script indicates naturalness and honesty. A signature written in a totally different style of writing to that in the main body of the script indicates shrewdness, cunning or possibly a mental disorder.

Fig. 49. An ornate signature indicating egoism.

Fig. 50. A simple signature indicating modesty.

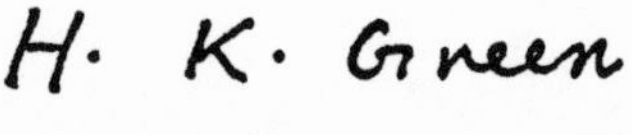

Fig. 51. A strikingly legible signature indicating pedantry.

Fig. 52. The signature of someone who wishes to be impenetrable.

CHAPTER 21

POSITIONS OF ENVELOPE ADDRESSES

Mental balance is indicated by an address centrally placed. Deviations are symbolised correspondingly as noted below.

Area ACDH. The projection of the super-ego and the equivalent to the upper zone of writing.

Area HDEG. The projection of the id and equivalent to the lower zone of writing.

Area ABFG. The projection of conservative, introvert tendencies and equivalent to a left-hand slope in writing.

Area BCEF. The projection of radical, extrovert tendencies and equivalent to a right-hand slope in writing.

Slightly to the left and right of the line BXF. The projection of independent, neutral tendencies and equivalent to upright writing.

Slightly above and below the line HXD. The projection of the ego and its relation to society; equivalent to the middle zone of writing.

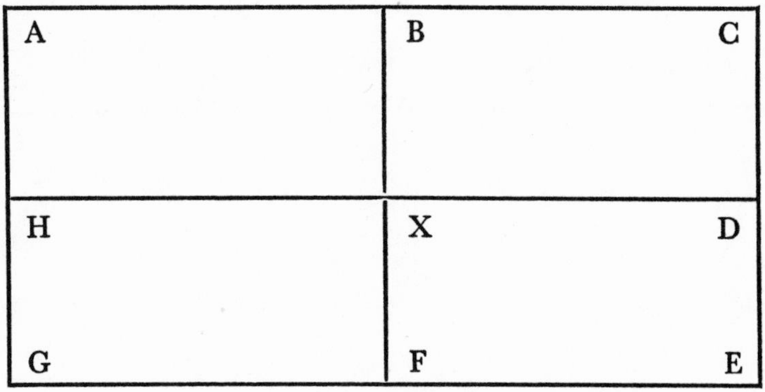

Fig. 53. Positions of envelope addresses.

Area ABXH. Indicates difficulty in social mixing, influence of the past and lack of faith in the future.

Area HXFG. Indicates caution, suspicion and inhibition of instinct.

Area BCDX. Indicates independence and strong activity but with little control.

Area XDEF. Indicates radicalism, action and materialism.

CHAPTER 22

CAPITAL LETTERS

Large capital letters can be interpreted positively as pride or negatively as pomp.

Christian names which begin with large capital letters indicate egocentricity or immaturity.

Surnames which begin with large capital letters can be interpreted positively as in-group pride (clan feeling) or negatively as a constant discrimination in favour of one's family.

In the illustrations below will be found certain varieties of formation of capital letters together with the appropriate interpretation.

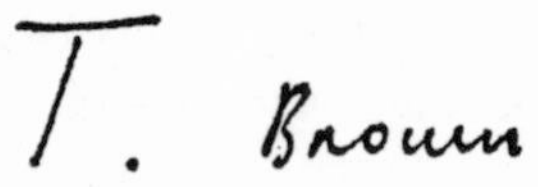

Fig. 54. Large capital initial of Christian name.

Fig. 55. Large capital initial letter of surname.

Narrow capital letter indicates
inhibition or shyness.

 Wide capital letter indicates
spontaneity and constructiveness.

 Complete block capital letter indicates
culture and thoroughness.

 Capital letter composed of over-
lapping strokes indicates lack of
thoroughness and lack of convention.

 Broken capital letter indicates
indiscretion and lack of thoroughness.

*Fig. 56. Varieties of formation of capital letters with appropriate
interpretations.*

Full middle zone with extension to the left : self-importance.

Extension in upper zone : initiative.

Left enrollment in middle zone : egoism.

Right enrollments in middle and upper zones : egoism, shrewdness.

Concave arc : constructiveness.

Fig. 57. Variation in formation of capital letters with appropriate interpretations.

Initial stroke and enrollment :
a calculating mind.

Underlining : self-love.

Wavy strokes : sense of humour.

Left arc at base : deceit,
irresponsibility.

Shorter second stroke :
ambition.

*Fig. 58. Variation in formation of capital letters with appropriate
interpretations.*

Right extension at base: defence taking the form of aggression.

Right extension into upper and lower zones: inferiority complex.

Left extension into upper and lower zones: superiority complex.

Right extension in upper zone: protecting spirit.

Fig. 59. Variation in formation of capital letters with appropriate interpretations.

Dollar sign : money-minded.

 Two crossing strokes : definiteness, exactness, aggression.

Fig. 60. Variation in formation of capital letters with appropriate interpretations.

CHAPTER 23

SMALL LETTERS

In the illustrations below will be found certain varieties of formation of small letters together with the appropriate interpretations.

 First part higher than second :
curiosity.

 Terminal stroke extending upwards
and to the left : misrepresentation
of facts.

⊃ ⊂ Two separate parts : inexactness,
talkativeness.

Fig. 60A. Variation in formation of small letters with appropriate interpretations.

Open at the top: talkativeness.

Open at the bottom: deceit.

Drawn to the left and open: unreliability.

Commencing stroke is nicked: hyper-sensitiveness.

Angle in upper and lower zones: analytical mind, resentfulness, lack of compromise.

Fig. 61. Variation in formation of small letters with appropriate interpretations.

CHAPTER 24

THE LETTER "I"

The letter "i" refers to our ego or, as we say, "number one". The way we write this particular letter symbolises our attitudes concerning our ego. A study of the variations in capital and small letter formation of this letter is so important as to justify a separate treatment from the other letters of the alphabet.

/   Plain capital : sense of essentials.

   Capital with full upper zone :
strong egoism.

    Capital with full upper zone and
enrolled lower zone : egoism, greed
and shrewdness approaching megalomania.

I   Printed capital : cultural interests.

*Fig. 62. Variations in formation of capital "I" with appropriate
    interpretations.*

Small letter with dot placed to
the left: caution.

Small letter with dot placed
exactly above: precision.

Small letter with dot placed to
the right: impulsiveness.

Small letter with dot missing:
unreliability, irresponsibility,
carelessness.

*Fig. 63. Variations in formation of small "i" with appropriate
    interpretations.*

Small letter with dot placed high :
idealism with possible unrealism.

Small letter with dot placed low :
materialism and realism (emphasised
if dot is heavy).

Small letter with dot in form of
accent : criticism.

Small letter with dot in form of
arcade : tact, deceit.

Small letter with faint dot :
poor vitality.

*Fig. 64. Variations in formation of small "i" with appropriate
interpretations.*

Small letter with dot in form of
arc open to left : neuroticism.

Small letter with dot in form of
arc open to right : observation.

Small letter with dot in form of
circle : escapism, eccentricity.

Fig. 65. Variations in formation of small "i" with appropriate interpretations.

CHAPTER 25

THE LETTER "T"

The letter "t", although not of the same degree of importance as the letter "i", is also justified in being treated separately from the rest of the alphabet since this letter enables us to symbolise our attitudes in ways that the other letters do not permit us to do.

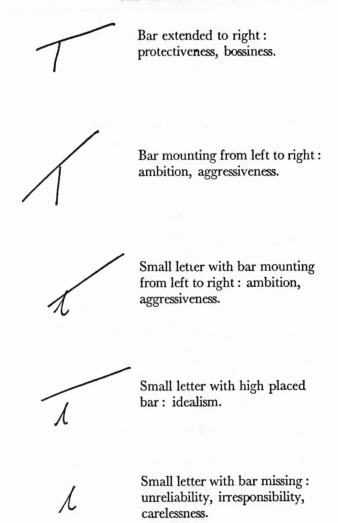

Bar extended to right:
protectiveness, bossiness.

Bar mounting from left to right:
ambition, aggressiveness.

Small letter with bar mounting
from left to right: ambition,
aggressiveness.

Small letter with high placed
bar: idealism.

Small letter with bar missing:
unreliability, irresponsibility,
carelessness.

Fig. 66 Variation in formation of capital and small "t" with appropriate interpretations.

Small letter with bar placed at top: ambition, bossiness.

Small letter with bar placed to left: caution.

Small letter with bar placed to right: impulsiveness.

Small letter with loop in upper zone: conceit.

Small letter with bar placed rather low: subordination.

Fig. 67. Variation in formation of small "t" with appropriate interpretations.

CHAPTER 26

INITIAL AND TERMINAL LETTERS

Initial and terminal letters of words are important in graphological study. This is because the execution of the strokes of these letters exhibits characteristics which are not so easily exhibited by the intervening letters of a word.

Some graphological practitioners believe that *every* initial letter indicates how the writer reacts to starting something. But the late Dr. George Strelisker did not believe this. He was of the opinion that only the *first letter of the first word* in a script indicated the writer's reaction to starting something new. Otherwise all other first letters of succeeding words were actually influenced by the last letters of preceding words. By this he meant that the space between words was more than an empty space—it constituted an "unwritten writing" in terms of the movements of the pen between the written words. However, this difference of opinion between graphologists does not lessen the importance of initial and terminal letters. On the contrary, the views of Strelisker give a new depth and meaning to the concept of writing as a dynamic system of flows.

But, to return to more practical matters, below are illustrations of the variations of initial and terminal letter formation.

Capital "A" starting with arc to left: greed.

Capital "A" ending with enrollment: egoism.

Small "b" starting with extended stroke from under base: aggressive activity.

Small "c" starting with extension from left: pull of the past.

Small "f" with repeated attempts to start: obsessions, self-doubts.

Small "g" starting with a black spot: "skeleton in the cupboard".

Fig. 68. Variations in initial letters with appropriate interpretations

Small "m" with normal execution:
normal sociality.

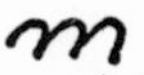

Small "m" with no end stroke:
asociality, anti-sociality, meanness.

Small "m" with terminal stroke
extended to right: sociality,
generosity.

Small "m" with terminal stroke
extended far to right: sociality,
compulsive hospitality, compulsive
social adjustment.

Small "m" with terminal stroke
extended into upper zone:
religious tendencies, mysticism.

*Fig. 69. Variations in terminal letters with appropriate
interpretations.*

Small "m" with terminal stroke
extending into upper zone to
form a loop: poetic appreciation,
imagination.

Small "m" with terminal stroke
extending into upper zone with
leftward turn to roof the word:
fatherliness, protectiveness.

Small "m" with terminal stroke
extending into upper zone with
leftward turn to roof terminal
letter only: factual misrepresentation.

Small "m" with terminal stroke
extending into upper zone with
leftward turn ending in a dot:
calculating flattery.

Small "m" with terminal stroke
extending into lower zone in form
of arcade: defensiveness,
unapproachableness.

Small "m" with terminal stroke
extending into lower zone with
force: uncompromising nature,
temper, aggressiveness.

*Fig. 70. Variation in terminal letters with appropriate
    interpretations.*

Small "m" with terminal stroke broad and extended to right: brutality.

Small "m" with terminal stroke weak and extended into lower zone: fatigue, low vitality.

Small "m" with terminal stroke extending to right and ending in a hook: obstinacy.

Small "m" with terminal stroke ending with less pressure and pointed: vindictiveness, sadism, sarcasm.

Fig. 71. Variations in terminal letters with appropriate interpretations.

CHAPTER 27

LOOPS IN THE LOWER ZONE

It is important to know something about the instincts of a writer of a particular script. Why? Because we then know something about the distribution of the writer's libido and the objects of his libido, that is to say, we can say what are the things or people or ideas which make life meaningful to him. In other words, what is it that interests the writer most in life? Perhaps it is nothing at all. Well, it is important to know these matters and we can know about them by a study of the loops of the lower zone, since the lower zone symbolises the sphere of the instincts.

For this purpose a study of the letters "f", "g", "y", "z" is most suitable. However, because of limitations of space, we shall confine our attention to a consideration of the variations of loop formation of the letter "g" with appropriate interpretations. The examples below will illustrate our considerations.

Small "g" normally executed:
normal erotic fixation and normal
degree of aggressiveness.

Small "g" with terminal stroke
slightly extended to right:
slightly excessive degree of
aggressiveness.

Small "g" with terminal stroke
fully extended to right: excessive
degree of aggressiveness.

Small "g" with terminal stroke
extended in lower zone to form
large loop: strong sexual
imagination.

Small "g" with terminal stroke
extended deep into lower zone to
form loop: strong sexual imagination.

*Fig. 72. Variations in lower zone loops with appropriate
interpretations.*

Small "g" with middle and lower
zone loops filled in:
sensuality.

Small "g" with no loop in lower
zone : fatalism, sense of essentials,
cultural sublimation.

Small "g" with underlength
uncrossed: disturbances in sex
life.

Small "g" with underlength
terminating in a leftward arcade:
deceit, irresponsibility.

*Fig. 73. Variations in lower zone loops with appropriate
interpretations.*

Small "g" with terminal stroke
in form of figure eight:
disturbances in sex life of
females, projection of female
components in males.

Small "g" with terminal strokes
in form of a triangle: hen-pecker.

Small "g" with terminal strokes
in form of triangle: strong
sense of reality, materialism.

Small "g" broken in two and with
terminal stroke without a loop:
neglect, unreliability,
dishonesty.

*Fig. 74. Variations in lower zone loops with appropriate
interpretations.*

CHAPTER 28

INTELLIGENCE

Intelligence is not a single ability. It is an over-all pattern composed of many parts. These parts consist of memory, imagination, intuition, reason, creation, invention, assimilation, co-ordination, etc. Thus, it will be obvious that intelligence cannot be evaluated by a single sign. Rather must many signs be taken into consideration. However, in any assessment of the intelligence of a writer the following points must be kept in mind :

(a) originality,
(b) good distribution of spaces,
(c) simplification,
(d) fluency,
(e) curves,
(f) speed,
(g) smallness,
(h) clever joining-up of "i"-dots and of "t"-bars with the succeeding letters,
(i) balance and proportion between the zones.

CHAPTER 29

UNRELIABILITY AND DISHONESTY

Unreliability or dishonesty, like intelligence, is not a single disability. It, too, is an over-all pattern composed of many parts. These parts consist of deceit, indecision, selfishness, materialism, etc. Thus, it will be obvious that unreliability or dishonesty cannot be evaluated by a single sign. Rather must many signs be taken into consideration. However, in any diagnosis of dishonesty or of unreliability in a script the following points must be kept in mind:

(a) lack of originality,
(b) artificiality and stylishness,
(c) poor distribution of spaces,
(d) impeded flow,
(e) arcades or angles (sometimes threads),
(f) slowness,
(g) ambiguity in letter execution,
(h) covering strokes,
(i) enrollments (especially in initial and terminal strokes),
(j) broken letters, letters with missing parts,
(k) frequent starts of the initial stroke,
(l) unnecessary touching-up of script in a vain attempt to improve legibility,
(m) missing letters,
(n) middle zone loops open at the base,
(o) left tendencies (especially in initial and terminal strokes),
(p) double loops in middle zone,
(q) exaggerations (especially in signature, capitals, loops, pressure),
(r) illegibility and a leftward slant,
(s) marked difference between script and signature,
(t) mixed writing system in an artificial script,
(u) writing of wrong letters and words (especially with an experienced writer).

However, it must be stressed that at least six of the above points should be noted in any one script before the possibility of dishonesty is seriously considered. This is necessary because many honest people make use of one or two of the above points.

CHAPTER 30

TRAIT LIST

Activity: firm downstroke; angular form, speedy.

Adaptability: even pressure; moderate speed; curved forms; garlands.

Aesthetic taste: good distribution of spaces; printed letters (especially capitals).

Affectation: ornamentation; large capitals; full loops.

Aggressiveness: heavy pressure; angles; speedy.

Ambition: rising "t"-bars; rising lines; extensions into upper and lower zones; even pressure; speedy; large capitals.

Amiability: garlands; right slope; low "t"-bars; fluency.

Anger: "t"-bars and terminal strokes heavy; high and pointed.

Apprehensiveness: up-strokes broken in upper zone.

Assertiveness: "t"-bars downwards or pointed; open ovals; large capitals.

Brutality: terminal stroke broadening.

Calmness: even pressure; slowness; curves; "i"-dots and "t"-bars placed low.

Carefulness: slowness; even pressure; regular spacing; legibility; exact "i"-dots and "t"-bars.

Carelessness: uneven pressure; irregular spacing; illegibility; misplaced or omitted "i"-dots and "t"-bars.

Caution: initial adjustments; closed ovals; dashes in place of periods; "i"-dots and "t"-bars light and/or replaced.

Ceremoniousness: artificiality; sham originality; flourishes; large capitals.

Clarity of thought: good distribution of spaces.

Coarseness: heavy pressure; ink blots; ungraceful forms.

Coldness: backward slant; sharpness.

Conceit: flourishes (especially in signature); large capitals; artificiality.

Concentration: small script; short extensions in upper and lower zones; "i"-dots and "t"-bars placed low.

Conscientiousness: sharpness; legibility; "i"-dots and "t"-bars placed low.

Constructiveness; originality; printed letters; use of concave.

Courage: good distribution of spaces; heavy pressure (especially with terminal strokes).

Cruelty: heavy pressure; pasty; terminals pointed and downward; "i"-dots and "t"-bars heavy and pointed.

Culture: printed letters; naturalness; originality.

Cunning: slowness; artificiality; upright or leftwards; mixed writing systems; ambiguity.

Curiosity: letters of middle zone pointed at top; "i"-dots and "t"-bars placed high.

Deceit: irregular base line; ambiguity; "d" and "o" open at base.

Depression: descending line; terminal stroke of last letter extended weakly into lower zone.

Determination: heavy pressure; heavy pressure of "t"-bars and terminal strokes ends abruptly; angles.

Diplomacy: closed ovals; upright script; artificiality; terminal letter diminishing.

Directness: simplification; omission of initial strokes.

Dishonesty: see pages 85, 86.

Dominativeness: large capitals; long and heavy "t"-bars; regular script.

Eccentricity: highly individualised script; unusual punctuation; ornamentation; artificiality.

Egoism: large capitals; flourishes and underlinings (especially in signature); enrollments to left; very full capital "I"'s.

Energy: angles; firm downstrokes; heavy pressure.

Ennui: slow; descending lines; descending "t"-bars and "i"-dots; low pressure in irregular script.

Enthusiasm: pressure rather heavy; speed rather fast; lines ascending; "t"-bars high-placed, long, ascending.

Exaggeration: large capitals; flourishes; large script; "i"-dots and "t"-bars placed high; extensions into upper and lower zones inflated.

Excitability: irregular script; "i"-dots and "t"-bars high placed in form of dashes.

Extravagance: wide spacing; large writing; wide margins or widening margins.

Fearfulness: upstrokes broken in upper zone; low pressure; narrow spacing.

Friendliness: garlands; naturalness; right slant; right extension.

Generosity: right extension of terminal strokes; wide spacing of words.

Honesty: see pages 85, 86.

Humour: horizontal strokes wavy.

Hypocrisy: "d" and "o" open at base; irregular base line.

Idealism: emphasis on upper zone.

Imagination: emphasis on upper zone; "i"-dots and "t"-bars placed high.

Impatience: angles; right slope; "i"-dots and "t"-bars placed to right.

Inactivity: slow; curves.

Independence: first strokes of "M" "N" "W" are higher than remaining strokes; angles; large capitals.

Instability: heavy pressure in irregular script; "i"-dots and "t"-bars placed high in form of dashes; variable speed.

Intelligence: see page 84.

Intuition: disconnected script.

Irresolution: rather slow script; variable placing of "i"-dots and "t"-bars; variable pressure and slant.

Irritability: angles; high placed "i"-dots and "t"-bars; variable height of letters.

Miserliness: narrow spacing between words and lines; no margins; terminal strokes short or hooked.

Modesty: simplification; naturalness; small script; small capitals.

Nervousness: sudden changes in speed, size, pressure.

Observation: small script; first stroke of "r" is higher than second; letter "e" shaped concave.

Obstinacy: heavy pressure; "t"-bars heavy and hooked; terminal strokes accentuated and hooked.

Optimism: lines and "t"-bars ascending.

Orderliness: good distribution of spaces; even margins; regular script.

Originality: legible deviations from the copy-book.

Patience: "i"-dots and "t"-bars placed low and exactly; curves; slow.

Perception: placing of "i"-dots and "t"-bars causes letter connections to be broken; good vertical spacing; small script; rather fast.

Practicality: terminal strokes short; narrow margins; narrow spacing between words; exaggerated extensions in lower zone; curtailed extensions in upper zone.

Procrastination: rather slow; "i"-dots and "t"-bars placed to left of stroke.

Reasoning: letters and words connected.

Resolution: rather fast script; "i"-dots and "t"-bars placed heavy and firm (accentuated by hooks).

Selfishness: see Egoism.

Sensitiveness: pressure in an irregular script; extreme right slant; wavering lines.

Sensuality: fullness in lower zone; pasty script; ink-filled loops.

Shrewdness: Enrollments; speedy; terminal strokes short; closed ovals.

Sincerity: see pages 85, 86.

Spirituality: exaggerated extensions in upper zone; light pressures; sharpness.

Stability: even pressure in regular script; "i"-dots and "t"-bars placed low and firm; steady speed.

Stupidity: see page 84.

Subordination: light pressure; curves; small capitals; "i"-dots and "t"-bars low placed.

Tactlessness: open ovals; terminal letters increasing.

Versatility: disconnected script; originality.

Vitality: narrow right margin; pressure in an irregular script; sharpness.

Vulgarity: artificiality; ornamentation; heavy pressure.

Weakness: low pressure in an irregular script; right tendencies in middle zone.

Will Power: heavy pressure in a regular script; firm strokes; heavy "i"-dots and "t"-bars; large size in a regular script; high pressure in a regular script.

RECORD OF A HANDWRITING ANALYSIS

Surname ....

Christian name(s) ....

Date of birth.....................	Sex...............................
Occupation	Nationality ....
Married or single	Family ....
Form level.......................	Predominant zone..............
Direction/slant	Width/narrowness ....
Word and line spacing.........	Connections ....
Direction of lines	Regularity/irregularity.........
Size	Pressure.........................
Pastiness/sharpness	Fullness/
Ornamentation/	leanness...........................
Simplification.....................	Left/right tendencies
Speed.............................	in zones ....
Signature	Margins..........................
Capital letters....................	Address position.................
Letter "i"	Small letters ....
Initial strokes....................	Letter "t" ....
Loops in lower zone............	Terminal strokes ....
Reliability	Intelligence ....

Summary ....

....

....

....

....

TABLE OF CHARACTERISTICS

Positive	Negative
adaptability	superficiality
altruism	utopianism
ambition	power mania
analytical-mindedness	criticism
anger	viciousness
broad-mindedness	vulgarity
constancy	dullness
colourful speech and manner	bombast
coolness	coldness
countryside interests	earthiness
carefulness	nervousness
caution	suspicion
dreaminess	distraction
determination	rigidity
diplomacy	insincerity
dexterity	cunning
economy	avarice, greed
excitability	hysteria
enthusiasm	excitability
energy	restlessness
endurance	fanaticism
emotional control	coldness
elasticity	inconstancy
enjoyment of living	lack of spirituality
ethical behaviour	asceticism
eroticism	perversion
ethical demands	neurotic conscience
family pride	exclusiveness
formality	vanity, isolation
femininity	yieldingness
firmness	hardness
fatigue	feebleness

Positive	*Negative*
generosity	lavishness
impulsiveness	irritability
independence	asociality, anti-sociality
intuitive thinking	lack of concentration
informality	familiarity
impressionability	superficiality
imagination	day-dreaming
kindness	suggestibility
loyalty	uncompromising nature
masculinity	awkwardness
maturity	lack of form sense
modesty	timidity
method	pedantry
naturalness	earthiness, rashness
originality	eccentricity
orderliness of thinking	lack of spontaneity
optimism	unrealism
open-mindedness	indecision
precaution	withdrawal
passion	emotional extravagance
progressiveness	radicalism
pessimism	depression
pride	pomp
rationality	lack of imagination, coldness
realism	pessimism
reserve	distrust
reproductive intelligence	lack of initiative
respectfulness	traditionalism
resoluteness	aggressiveness
sensitivity	weakness
sensuality	crudeness
spirituality	asceticism
self-discipline	coldness
sociability	compulsive hospitality
social success	social climbing
social discrimination	snobbishness
sensuousness	addiction
sublimation	suppression, repression
simplicity	neglect
steadiness	inertia

thoughtfulness	slowness of thought
taste	artificiality
tactfulness	insincerity
tolerance	indifference
traditionalism	fear of the future
uncommittedness	indifference
vitality	excitability
vision	utopianism
vivacity	escapism
warm nature	amiability

BIBLIOGRAPHY

Becker, M., *Graphologie der Kinderhandschrift*, Frieburg, 1926.

Brooks, C. H., *Your Character from Your Handwriting*, London, 1946.

Bunker, M. N., *Case Book Number One*, American Institute of Grapho-analysis, Kansas City, 1936.

Crépieux-Jamin, J., *L'Ecriture et le Caractere*, Paris, 1888.

Crépieux-Jamin, J. *ABC de la Graphologie*, Paris, 1930.

Duparchy Jeannez, M., *L'Expression de Maladie Dans L'Ecriture*, Paris.

Jacoby, H., *Analysis of Handwriting*, London, 1939.

Jacoby, H., *Handschrift und Sexualitaet*.

Klages, L. R., *Einfuehrung in die Psychologie der Handschrift*, Heilbronn, 1924.

Klages, L. R., *Handschrift und Charakter*, Leipzig, 1940.

Langenbruch, M., *Praktische Menschenkenntnis auf Grund der Handschrift*, Berlin, 1929.

Lombroso, C., *Handbuch der Graphologie*, Leipzig, 1902.

Mendel, A. O., *Personality in Handwriting*, New York, 1947.

Mendelsohn, A. and G., *Der Mensch in der Handschrift*, Leipzig, 1928.

Meyer, G., *Wissenschaftliche Grundlagen der Graphologie*, Jena, 1925.

Morf, G., *Praktische Charakterkunde*, Bern, 1945.

Myer, O. N., *The Language of Handwriting*, London, 1958.

Pulver, M., *Symbolik der Handschrift*, Zürich, 1945.

Pulver, M., *Intelligenz im Schriftausdruck*, Zürich.

Pulver, M., *Trieb und Verbrechen in der Handschrift*, Zürich, 1934.

Rand, A., *Graphology*, London, 1962.

Roman, K. G., *Handwriting: A Key to Personality*, London, 1954.

Saudek, R., *The Psychology of Handwriting*, London, 1928.

Saudek, R., *Experiments with Handwriting*, London, 1928.

Schermann, R., *Die Schrift Luegt Nicht*, Berlin, 1929.

Schneidemuehl, G., *Handschrift und Charakter*, Leipzig, 1911.

Singer, E., *The Graphologist's Alphabet*, London, 1950.

Singer, E., *Personality in Handwriting*, London, 1954.

Sonnemann, U., *Handwriting Analysis*, New York, 1950.

Strelisker, G., *Das Erlebnis der Handschrift*, Steyermühl-Verlag, Leipzig, Vienna, Berlin, 1934.

Wolff, W., *Diagrams of the Unconscious*, New York, 1948.

Wormser, P., *Die Beurteilung der Handschrift in der Psychiatrie.*